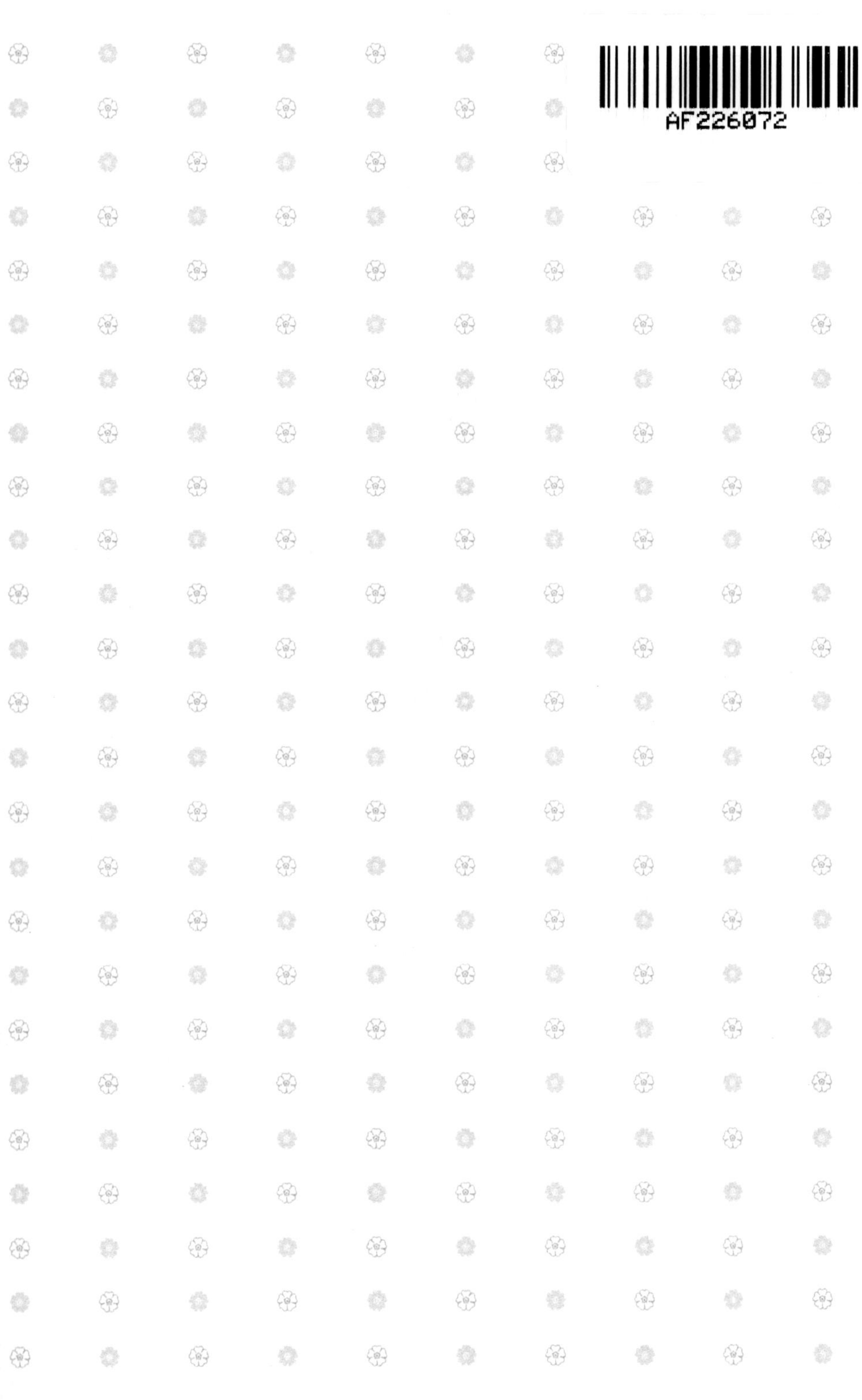
AF226072

in case of emergency press

We are proud to acknowledge the Traditional Owners of
country throughout Australia and to recognise their
continuing connection to land, waters, and culture.
We pay our respects to their Elders.

We support recognition, reconciliation, and reparation.

Symphonie Disharmonica

Mukund Gnanadesikan

in case of emergency press
https://icoe.com.au
Travancore, Victoria
Australia

Published by in case of emergency press 2026

ISBN: 978-1-7637749-8-8

Cover design: Ward Nikriph

Acknowledgements

Versions of the following poems were first published in the following journals:

"A Long Time Coming"- Ginosko
"A Question of Identity", "When He's Had Enough"- Fevers of the Mind
"Beside the Inferno"- The Hellebore
"Cinco De Mayo", "Detention"- Tuck Magazine
"Conscientious Objector", "Empathy and Skepticism", "Smolder"- Unlikely Stories
"Egret"- Door is a Jar
"El Campesino Orgulloso"- The Abstract Elephant
"El Viaje Peligroso"- Crepe and Penn
"Lines"- Junto Magazine
"Lûc Bat for the Ancestors- Angel Island 2022"- Provenance
"Neighbors"- Stardust Review
"Oscar"- The Cape Rock
"Somewhere Soon, USA"- Duck Lake Journal
"Southern Cross"- Poesis (now W-Poesis)
"Strangers"- Poetry Quarterly
"The Arrival"- The Poet Magazine Adversity Anthology
"The Gravedigger's Arithmetic", "Observations on Collective Self-Occultation"- Querencia Press
"The Last Days of Tyranny"- New Verse News
"Unlucky"- Adelaide Literary Magazine
"Visibility"- Flumes Literary Magazine
"White Lies", "Speaking in Tongues'- Cordite Poetry Review
"War Wounds"- Praxis
"World Sickness"- POETiCA Review

I owe a collective debt of gratitude to the editors of all the above publications.

Dedication

To my family, especially my wife Dominik

Table of Contents

Symphonie Disharmonica

Mukund Gnanadesikan

SONATA

The Gravedigger's Arithmetic

In the beginning, the sum of my knowledge was nil.
Then came subtraction,
the family integer minus one
equaling an unnatural number.

And minus one and two and four—
genocide's obliteration is asymptotic.
One body, and one body, and one body
became eight, then sixteen, then a village.

Mourning is geometric progression,
nothing common in its ratio,
the calculus of corpse-makers.
Demagogues divide, invoking imaginary integers.

Coruscated parabolas rebuff integration.
Incendiary arcs whine and whistle,
foundations shake and fracture
shaken by wrathful throbs of a sinusoidal pulse.

In enmity's infinite ouroboros
we draw no tangents.
In the bitter smoke, sine waves of sound become inaudible:
amplitude, frequency, attributes we don't possess.

And in the papers, black and white,
we are reduced to two dimensions,
finite brown knobs on an abacus,
dependent variables of combustible thermodynamics.

Half-mast in the Aftermath—A Poem for Uvalde

Old Glory is a flogged feline, mewling.

Yet even cats perceive injustice,

bemoan burgundy spatter

diffused on a brick wall, marked on a concrete sidewalk.

Hardiness and valor hemorrhage,

staining alabaster innocence.

See jagged borders blur, fibers fray—

A banner oft-defiled no longer flaps.

Look closely, scrutinize those stars.

No longer heavenly, they smell of scalded flesh,

punctured to admit onrushing tides of grief,

the wind's sad stirring of a falling flagpole.

Star Spangles

Rockets' red glare
leave carmine grief
in sooty trails.

Drunken giants
stand triumphant,
heads held aloft.

Barbarism,
cold tragedy
or victory?

Cold, somber eyes
see only fog:
Empathy melts.

Conscientious Objector

I shall not unfurl these fists.
To do so means expungement of my neighbor
and never have I closed another's eyelids,
cut the taut hawser

that tethers him to identity's pier.
I will not burn our common harvest.
Not in the waning light of day, or at cock-crow.
I'd sooner stand here, quebracho-stiff,

your barrel to my ear,
than detonate
incendiary tools of bloodshed.
Platinum valor gleams

even under gunfire,
ceding no domain.
Melt your rifles on the seething coals.
Stare down the tanks with me, upon the cobblestones.

Strangers

We lie prostrate, splayed upon beaches,
caked with white sand.
Drawing labored breaths,
lonely but lachrymose,
we do not move, but for moistened cloths
waving plaintive fishtail ends

in doleful eddies.
Huddled on a lifeboat,
Terror begat Hope,
but Hope's quixotic
heartbeat
is arrested and arrhythmic.

No banners droop for us,
no laments recall inflections unfamiliar.
See the phantom spirits, darkened skins
shrinking beneath a nation's mushroom cloud.
Go ahead, avert your eyes from us.

Your courage has fled south for winter.
So too has compassion.
How else shall we explain
rimy indifference
to swollen bellies, broken bones?

Numb your ears
to the cautery of a mother's wail.
Shut your callous, jaundiced eyes.
What you choose not to perceive
will throw you from your perch.

Oscar

Headed home to see my girl;
just a black feather on bay winds.
Family, that's what important.

Johannes, why the gun?
Waiting for a train, I'm a seagull
looking for a killifish, no bad intentions.

What makes you bend your index finger,
sending metal teeth
into my tender skin?

What did you see—a cobra in my jaw,
a lion in the twitch of a brown thumb?
Were you scared?

Blackness has that effect sometimes
on panicked hands
endowed with loaded weapons.

The Last Days of Tyranny

In the capital city, mustachioed Napoleon
wields his Kalashnikov
peacocking, bedecked in finery, touting his potency,
knowing he is but a puffer fish.

The coalescing crowds metamorphose,
now a famished tiger shark.
He must depart, fade into shadows
lest the blood that flows will spring from his own pump.

Uniformed lackeys stand aside, listening:
the clamor of millions chanting, a civic tsunami.
The square's crescendo separates a strongman from his rifle.
The many shall consume the one.

Behold the rise of the agora.
Let sentiment engrave in stone
collective will and testament.

Observations on Collective Self-Occultation

Trapped between faith's boulder
and a cracked cement foundation
in a moment of annularity,
we risk eclipse
under acrid showers of white phosphorus,
and whining rockets whistling overhead.

Let oval rings of fire delineate
a common boundary,
encourage circumferential joining.
Walk the perimeter, hand in steady hand.
Clear the air of cacophonous cries,
let symphonies of thrush and wren return.

El Campesino Orgulloso
(The Proud Farmworker)

Consider now the humble *campesino*,
who minds green vines with periwinkle love,
not pausing to enjoy nectarous flowers
that stand vigilant in rose-oil memorial.
Who knows if trailing plants grow proudly?
But with the proper nurture they grow ancient.

The texts ignore sudoric labor, crystalline and ancient.
While nobles quaff merlot, the *campesino*
heaves without complaint, wears thorn-scars proudly,
or so we say with feigned respect and love.
And after death, no headstone, no memorial
for the indefatigable, barebone-grey beneath the flowers.

Eyes closed, the worker dreams of flowers,
a blooming field where grandchildren strut proudly.
At the green's center, by the memorial,
tourists pose for pictures, commemorating love.
And from this dream awakes the *campesino*
whose steady hand sustains the vineyard ancient.

Inebriated visitors defile the stone memorial,
sanding down the topography of love.
Light still breathes in heart of *campesino*,
his loyalty to earth as ancient
as tears or laughter, dung or flowers.
Forehead to the sunlight, he sacrifices proudly.

Beneath feudal lord's coercion, he plows on proudly,
each rectilinear furrow a welcoming memorial.
Plows and tractors furnish bacchanals of love
but tools mean nothing without *el campesino*
whose hands coax earth to yield gifts most ancient,
far older still than recurring annual flowers.

Rain showers and hallowed hands, ancient,
Liberate ebullient blooming flowers,
their ochre hues, humility flashed proudly.
Bowed heads. Respect the stone memorial.
Here we see the confluent vines of love,
made fruitful by constant *campesino*.

Rain garlands of red flowers on plots of love.
See the memorial, embrace it proudly.
Honor *campesino*'s earthly spirit, proud and ancient.

Textbooks of the 1980s

The words we read in books as children
were penned by blue-eyed men dyed ruddy pale.
Grandiose victors, bare-loined assassins of shadow lions:
all too human, they could not endure
the hail of arrows, stones, of bullets and of loss
sent by cavalier invaders who burned the fields of history.

All countries tout their brands: "our" people, history,
but "our" and "their" are false: we all were children,
some stripped of childhood by loss,
others by sight of corpses limp and ashen-pale.
How shall innocence endure
the ugly truth that all beasts yield to lions?

We fear the apex predators, the lions,
but sculpt them into obelisks of history.
Heirs of the vanquished must endure
the legacy of years, passed down to children
embalmed in tales of inhumanity beyond the pale,
white-washed impressionisms of their loss.

One nation's victory, another feels as loss.
Clans are dismembered by prides of frenzied lions.
Once green, the leaves are sickly pale.
The dying sunrays expose proud fools' history,
preserving softest glow for final games of children
hidden in corners, praying to endure.

Hope's candle will flicker, yet must endure,
as sure as freedom smooths the sandpaper of loss.
Winged fantasies of fairies comfort fearful children.
Imbibing lessons of adventure, saints and lions,
they too will be forgotten in sanitized history,
sterilized apocrypha of tawny men scrubbed pale.

At a father's grave, once-tanned cheeks now pale,
the son wonders how he can endure.
Empires sacrificed his lineage to history,
heedless of a village's loss.
Pompous leaders roar, soon sated like well-fed lion,
then close their eyes to orphaned children.

Paralyzed by soul-destroying loss,
helpless before God and man, we ask mercy of lions.
Someone, somewhere, save the children.

Southern Cross

Phosphorescent, volatile hatred
inflames citizens' hearts,

planted by vitriolic,
scarlet wrinkled hands.

Torch-bearing men
march, chanting mantras,

projecting holographic bravado,
frightened under ghost-sheets,

screaming of purity,
melting like slush.

Fools announce themselves,
impervious to logic.

Epidermis hides nothing
from educated eyes;

Show your faces.
We fear not.

Unity stands resolute.

Fermata #1

Orange poppies commingle
with red and yellow.
No conflict in the meadows,
no trace of bloodshed.

ANDANTE

Empathy and Skepticism
(erasure after Anthony Walton's "Dissidence")

You have to be the pain, imagine loneliness,

learn indifference to rain,

welcome noise like silence.

Sleep, trucks careening,

whining sirens mapping splintered intervals,

unafraid of dissonance, of resolution.

Disagree with the path you climb, the journey.

Distrust all you hear.

Speaking in Tongues

Your accent says you do not speak my language—
a barrier we never dare cross.

Who defines these borders, tells us not to cross?
Only fear's shadowy warning signs.

The timbre of your tongue is strange, a sure sign
you do not hail from here, my neighbors.

And here we are, eyes skeptical of neighbors
whose words transcend aural perception.

If shoes were switched, I would fear your perception.
Truth's needle stings my blackened conscience.

When I say, "Welcome", the voice is my conscience
attempting to put your mind at ease.

You have passed months in restless, lonely slumber.
No more. I'll learn to speak your language.

An Alternate Universe

Do not walk a mile in another's shoes
but wear his hide instead.

See wary wide-eyed glances, backward steps,
balled fists at the ready.

What do you see under the street lamps?
Behind you, tear gas seeps through the window.

Your searing lungs choke.
Rat-a-tat gunfire erupts—now do you understand?

Look below the surface: beneath a judge's robe,
a tight blue uniform, a gun and badge and truncheon.

Lines

Between unbending fences,
bleeding hearts etch indelible odes

in erasable ink: boldfaced lamentations
inscribed on brittle scrolls.

Frantic fingers seek forgiving cracks
in obdurate stone.

In the distance, a signboard's neon siren
promises cheap victuals.

In the foreground
a grimy cheeked infant

suckles barren breasts.
In minutes to hours, his lungs will fall silent.

Some leave, more stand on tiptoes,
peer across the stern partition.

Over the border, suspended on saguaros,
tattered banners wave.

El Viaje Peligroso
(The Dangerous Journey)

Cactus spines and heat will not defeat us,
though burnt skin peels
beneath a wrathful sun.

We mark out progress in lacerations
from the steel edge of a fence,
the thump of a *coyote*'s tight-balled fist.

Skin, no matter how tough, rips like oilcloth.
In the desert sun, generations perish,
but no blood dries in vain, *mi hijo*.

Always remember every wound.
Your future and my past link trembling fingers,
for in them now hope's hummingbird we hold.

War Wounds

Her first love pulls triggers for a living.
He never questions his commanders.
All doubts have been suppressed.
All orders must be followed.

Father watches rocket spirals on the news and shrugs:
"The poor boy made his choice."
The boy's betrothed recalls farewell embrace,
acerb despite his lilac pledge of marriage.

She waits at the window, a loyal hound, though fearful
of the black lace veil that now adorns
his sergeant's bereft wife, scrubbing away death's smirch.
sitting in a darkened house a thousand miles away.

Eyes closed, she wishes to erase
carmine tears from a copper land,
to bind the angry, greedy hands
that transmute leaden slugs to gold.

Detention

Her disarticulated life-limbs begs indulgence,
Intoning a harmonic plea in disconnected English,
entreating my unfamiliar, unskilled hands

to aid in reassembly of a macerated nest.
Mother-son bonds, adamantine,
were once unbreakable,

sealed by barnacle adhesive
of hands interlocked,
strengthened by legend, tradition,

common dreams palpable
in each metronomic heartbeat,
secreted from each pore.

I see her sacrifice, offering blood-stained droplets as alms.
Her heaving breaths prompt an apology,
a thin line in a whirlpool of depravity.

I alone will never be enough to salve her wounds.
Knowing this, I seek silken words of comfort,
wishing to be the knight who shatters dungeon walls,

reuniting a son with his dust bowl-battered mother.
Thirsty for justice, she wants more than words,
more than my frozen tongue can author.

I bear no succor
and she remains alone,
a gaunt kit fox, clinging to an empty water bottle.

Cinco De Mayo

He strolls into the classroom
wrapped in *El Tricolor*,
nods at his neighbor.
The teacher frowns,

thumps on his desk,
commanding, brow knitted,
"Take that off.
You're in America now."

Murmurs swell,
rippling rows of umber faces
a windblown sorghum field.
He lifts a finger to his lips.

Discarding the garment,
he stands stock-still,
immovable, touches his heart,
its unstoppable rhythm.

For Love of Money

Looming glass dragons
reflect foolish aspiration,
a haunted-house mirage
painted in red lipstick.

See the slate-eyed women
strutting prudently,
smooth ankles exuberant
atop polished marble floors.

The slack-faced guard
sips coffee picked last year
by a child on a Guatemalan *finca*.
A bare-chested street urchin looks on,

unaccompanied by guardians or luck,
face pressed against the glass,
dreaming of an advertisement's promises:
full belly, fuller pocket.

The tropical storm swirls between tall buildings
whose terraces gesture to heaven
but soon will launch a usurer
to well-earned ruin upon unyielding cobblestones.

Youthful Offender

Sourdough-faced, he sits before me.
Across the rusted metal table, dry oak-leaf eyes wallow
in the thick morass of sins long past, not easily forgotten.

I ask him why he's here.
He shrugs, "Wrong place, wrong time, doc.
I didn't mean no harm."

Absolution doesn't live here,
though by rights it owes you warmth
on pitted floors where generations lived to die.

I wonder what made you yield to darkness,
(or was it illness?) This is not for me to judge,
yet I indulge. My jury hangs:

beneath abhorrent deeds once lay a softness
though it has petrified by now.
Compassion knew your name, your mother says.

Within me, pity's firefly flickers, then decays.
Just so behind these bars, your eyes
are concrete chambers, where light rays fear to tread.

A Question of Identity

We refuse to blend
into the pink tropical sand.
Together, we stand out,
more visible than rocky cliffs
from which, facing the wind,
myrmecoid secrets of the past crawl into our ears.

Climb the ladder to the bluff,
sea grass stabs our shins;
we parry it away, offering nothing
but rejection as ancestors once did,
who stood guard upon this ledge
and threw tribes brown tribes

into a sea-green hereafter.
Our neighbors term this survival.
I declare it extinction.
And soon we all are gone,
no voices audible, nor footsteps,
not a scrap of sentimental cotton.

O dear Lord, please tell us who we are
and who we might have been.

When He's Had Enough

Today of all days, he stands, feet firmly planted.
A wide-based banyan, rooted in an urban forest,
rustling to the melodic susurrus of revolution.

This grove of thumping hearts,
of simmering polyphonic chants
like summer rain to a parched leaf,
strip away fear's binding web.

A dying town's cardia beats again.
Can this organ suction indignation
from diaphragm to mouth,
capillary of rebellion?

He moves nowhere, and never will,
though others fall earthward
beneath patrician smoke.

A Long Time Coming

In my swirling antebellum nightmares
I hear the auctioneer shout through his bullhorn:
"Greetings, gentlemen, and welcome
Today we have the world's finest stock
Fresh and exotic.

Behold these broad, sloping shoulders
thick-sinewed haunches
ridged with muscle,
prepared for faithful service
each for his purpose

in silent labor.
This fine specimen will never cry
whether under sun or lash.
There is something here
for every need that must be met."

Two centuries beyond,
though shackles rust
and chains have broken,
yet still today they gawk
at Black and Brownness,

as at a snorting Brahma bull.
And now I say to them:
Hear rebellion's drumbeat.
It swells and echoes, coming nearer.
Unwavering hands

reap equity's fiber
and long-withheld amends
from venerable cotton fields,
their deceptive softness
fertilized by forefathers' blood.

Unfettered bodies
run in unison, legs rippling
prideful voice raised aloud.
Silent obedience has gone extinct.
Your riot gear and dogs won't stem the rising tide.

Among the Monuments

There is no wholesome image here,
no child's delight of driven snow
to melt upon an outstretched tongue.

Behold the marble obelisks,
buffed to a lustrous, icy sheen,
all human flaws obscured, befogged

by ignorance's opium dream.
Imposing bronze erections rise
adhere each section to its base.

Here in the park, why do they stand,
these colonists and conquerors,
culprits of oxblood genocide?

Now let us topple history.
Yes, let us watch false idols burn,
and gleam in flaming consequence.

Smolder
(after Claude McKay's "The White House")

From this broken goblet,
I imbibe the sweet sap of your hate.
All men created equal–
an ignored truth inviolate.

Calmly, I simmer
my solitary discontent
while neighbors look askance,
sere covers draped on skeletal suspicions, unbent.

Not by content of character shall I be judged,
but by my face.
Calm, circumspect relatives,
smelling of camphor, speak of grace.

Their singsong words resonate.
I try to discern the faint tracks of their feet
up and down the trash-strewn alleys,
across the overflowing street

where the crowds swell, push shoulders, elbows,
squeeze through the narrow pass,
the hubbub interrupted
by shrill, sharp sundering of glass

upon dispassionate cement
packed with inhumanity at lunch hour.
I shall not fabricate a polished image,
better to stay raw.

as you shed my blood,
cut sinew, take my power,
please know this:
I will defy your arcane vestiges of law.

Fermata #2

White cloth kite waltzes
A dragon on a thin string
Beware fickle gusts

37

SCHERZO

NIMBY

The Undesirables, tied together
by the soiled hemp rope of slander,
are cast aside, discarded syllables
from a broken-legged stanza.

Not in our backyard, the neighbors say,
holding placards written in black ink,
outlined in fear's stark white border.
Those new brown bodies must go elsewhere.

Sure, someone must take care
of the sun-scarred men with muddy work boots,
women marked by the rounded bulge of future hope,
but they are shunned on the sidewalks.

And so, I stand here, in the cul-de-sac
screaming questions at a dormant god.
Why must the acid of self-interest
dissolve collective soul so quickly?

World Sickness

Empathy's stone-blocked arteries
strand children at water's edge,
folded in half, expiring from thirst.

Still focused on the mirror. we practice ignorance,
ignoble eyes averted from cachectic shadows,
glancing sideways with a shudder?

We choose our own fraternities
a smug tribe of zombie voyeurs,
anesthetized and humorless automatons.

A holiday's uplifting paeans
exalt disillusioned spirits
igniting hope's flickering candle.

Half-blind eyes look west to boastful peaks.
Under a salmon sky
Rushmore's idols crumble.

The Sit-In
(After Claude McKay's "If We Must Die")

We will not waver from this spot
though the police truss us like hogs,
though they send water cannons, slavering dogs.
You will understand, though many may not.

It is our lot to disintegrate the hardness of this world.
By the riverhead, remember whose blood was shed.
Honor life's legacy by studying your dead,
learn their lessons while you clutch your pearls,

and defy the covetous thunder-seizing foe.
Remember us. Inhale the oakmoss of the brave.
From first breaths to years enclosed in a blind grave
we have fought this war's decisive blow.

When we project our voices, they will hear.
Collective power makes oligarchs know fear.

The Arrival

She knows the hand held out can be withdrawn,
subject to fickle gusts of empathy.
Compassion's voice does not sing forever.
Samaritans retreat to crackling fires.

She knows this, supine on the itchy sand.
Her white blouse torn, her thinning hair salt-caked,
bony arms cradle the half-clad cherub
whose small but robust lungs demand redress.

Mother stretches, grasps for a small sandwich,
undoes its obstinate cocoon.
In halting words, she asks consecration
of watchful sinners now unduly blessed.

She swaddles the small babe in pilling wool;
Though safe for now, she dreads each passing hour.

Unlucky

The crookbacked cleaner hobbles
on the twisted ankle of ill circumstance.
Pain is nothing
if not constant in its attentions.

No arms extend to hold her,
to buttress a flimsy frame
thin as a communion wafer
and equally as disregarded.

She scrubs away the dirt, the dust,
makes ostentatious dwellings gleam.
Invisible, she disappears
with a twenty, no thank you from the boss.

Home is a dingy room, musty and sparse,
safe for the shedding of tears,
fit for little else.
Dare she ask for more?

Neighbors

Could I do more for you or you for me?
So insular our small adjacent worlds,
so little effort I made to know you.

I offer transparent indifference,
although you have a heart, aflush with dreams.
Why have I never even dared to ask?

Is it fear that raises picket fences,
reminds us not to touch low hanging plums?
Kronos, the dogged god of time

shambles behind at a constant tempo.
On the sidewalks, we listen to his steps.
A wave, a nod, and we return inside.

The white tulip of forgiveness soon wilts.
Harsh climes intrude to strip its petals off.
Prosperity decides to yield to jealous blight.

Where are *charizomai, aphiemi?*
Oh, rains of absolution, cleanse this soul,
scarred deeply by a hoary winter frost.

White Lies

The bovine smile upon my brown-skinned face
conceals fear and anger's boiling broth

      You greet me as you blow upon your broth
      You don't desire a genuine response

For many years I've sought the genuine response
Of actions matching full intent of eyes

      But deeds themselves discern intent of eyes
      And feed the senses poisoned nectar

So thirstily, we drink this poisoned nectar
Savoring blooms that slowly perish

      At different speeds, we all slowly perish
      A thorn of truth pierces joyful anthems

Wave your banners, sing loud your joyful anthems.
You'll hear nothing from my brown-skinned face.

Right of Way

Pock-marked gravel road,
a winding trail to nowhere,
scolds the footsteps of a child:
"Private Road – Keep out".

Tranquil wooded paths inspire an apoplectic tirade.
The old miser's ruddy fingers
clutch a deed to land inherited by blood,
property assigned over a native chieftain's corpse.

What's his is his, he shouts,
to hoard and stash away.
I ask if he inclines to fill temptation's gourd
with green and gold?

Go ahead, mister.
Cling to the leafy forest floor,
the murmuring river,
the osprey's nest atop a redwood platform.

Grasp your money tightly.
It will expire when you do.
In time you will be moss.
You will be meadow.

The waters will reproach you.
Time and property tumble,
possessions bruised by friction.
No canyons cry for pebbles in the river.

Luc Bát for the Ancestors—Angel Island 2022

See the peeling casern
Here guards loomed, taciturn, silent,

threatened frigid violence.
Free will, self-reliance not strong

but through this pent-up wrong,
their starving hearts bred song, soft *ge*[1].

Their heirloom poetry
becomes a tapestry of words.

Our legends will be heard.
Sylvan embers stirred, ignite,

and in the gloaming light,
ghosts crowded over-tight, enclosed.

And through the squall, God dozed,
but progenitors rose, still do—

a homeland's hymns they coo,
In a thicket of rue, they mourn.

---

[1] *A type of singing originating in Chinese Buddhism*

Visibility

Renown across the globe:
a roseate dream envisioned
by hungry eyes
whose dusky skin is shadowed.

Conceived and classified
he was always called "inferior",
cast out, shut out
by those who silence honesty,

veil images that glow too brightly.
Anthropic forces feel no pain
bulldozing human trunks, but tonight
angry lanterns chase averted eyes.

Let unrest's strong bellows fan flames
of golden furor
that leap to fullest height
in incomplete illumination.

Let us watch your shadows lengthen,
hear audacious anthems' crescendo.
Quaff the liquor of notes that crackle,
of pitches that burn.

Fermata #3

Lions, wildebeests
chase across the Kalahari,
all lives under siege

51

RONDO

52

Beached

Neophyte gray whale putrefies,
entrenched in Limantour's beige strand.

An unaccompanied minor
separated from the pod, misguided,

now lies naked to the ribs.
Decaying flesh admonishes

of suffocating ligatures,
the cruel sum of a dozen rainbow ribbons,

instruments of technicolor strangulation.
Its closed eye reproaches me

and in this moment, somewhere in the
amethyst bay, underwater baritone plays Taps,

a Cetacean saxophone arrangement
echoing aqueous elegy.

Here on the beach, as children gawk,
no final rites are given.

Compliance

To survive, bend: your tender stalk
will break beneath steel-toed boots,
the thunder of despotic fortune.

Lean with the prevailing winds:
a curtsy or bow
protects vital ratoons.

Drink humbly what is offered:
Heaven's cloudbursts, unearned
merit upturned leaves.

At sunset, close your greedy petals:
await morning's invitation.
Only Helios forgives daily desire.

Apostrophe for a Stray

What does this alley hold for you?
Does an overflowing dumpster,
its odorous maw protruding,
fulfill the promises of all you never had?

Sores riddle flea-ridden skin.
I say I understand
why you shrink into the corner,
whimpering when there is no retreat,

but I know nothing
of raspy lungs' desperate heave,
weeping excoriations,
a companionless demise.

I want to say, "Come with me,
I am nurturance and nourishment"
but the fervor in my breast is vapor-thin,
the faith behind your eyes a flimsy ghost.

The Destroyer

I walk down the golden strand.
The green-glass sea is a sapphire-tressed siren.
A camera-wielding tourist
watches his cellophane wrapper

floating on a summer gust.
Distracted by gyrating mermaid dancers,
he ignores plastic extrusions,
grants it liberty to roam the dunes.

Limbs and thought deny responsibility,
lacking indigo-violet colors of compassion
for sand and sea,
for birds and fish that feast.

How much can be expected
of human hearts that can't regale
what blinded eyes deny?
He strides away, bewitched by crashing waves,

but apathy's hypnotic flower
is opium for disillusionment.
Slumbering conscience bathed in gold
ignores the warning of the terns.

Equine Advisory

You stand before my stall,
forgetting I could break the door down
if I chose to. Count your blessings:
I accept it all, the saddle, bridle, bit.

Fully flexed pleasure
is scarce in the paddock.
I do not stretch my legs,
unless at your command.

You bid me trot in circles,
hurdle wooden barriers.
Passivity is what you want. I humor you.
I, the wild one, live at your caprice.

Indulge, oh hominid, the privilege of pride
washed down with foamy spirits—
I'll rest my haunches upon ticklish bedding,
a manger more Jesuit than yours.

A Natural Home

Every heartbeat sinks its attendant footprints
into proximal patches of dispassionate earth.

Opportunity is ownership.
Mine—

A word that sucks up maple sap,
drinks wetland marsh water.

Sentience means selfishness. Progress
equal entrails on a dune.

What is it we value,
illuminated under constellations?

Empty visions crave planar simplicity, building shelter,
though others' domiciles may fall to ashes.

Species and icecaps melt.
First Person Singular shall plant his flag.

The Ballad of *Rana Pipiens*

The mottled frog, first seen flattened,
dust-covered on the roadside shoulder,
remains unperturbed,
no longer showing any hint of green,

darkened by the arid climes and sunlight.
Humanity never paused
to offer respects to the cantor,
extinguished with the squish of a stolid tire track.

Better late than never, I reckon,
to localize eternal peace.
May I one day join his number,
another colored character melded with the dust.

To a Desert Hummingbird

Hover:
kiss the blushing barrel cactus,
syncopated fan-wings whirring,
perpetual helicopter blades,
your curvilinear feeding straw
a sinuous persuader.

Willing blooms and nectaries
lean forward to fulfill.
Never stationary,
incessant motion evades harshness,
locating dulcitude
between thorniest projections.

Egret

Evening tides bring fulfillment
(or so I presume)
watching you stand guard
in the waning light.

Atop a convex bridge span,
you assert avian supremacy,
perching here as your ancestors did.
SUVs careen past, ignoring your hegemony.

Their homeward rush
anticipates society's chaotic mating call.
A rusty sign warns
KEEP OUT, meant for me and my ilk.

Human intellect chooses not to honor you,
slave to mint's green currency.
Highways widen.
Marshlands lie void.

The mud-suckers have perished.
Fly away.

Beside the Inferno

Paradise is burning
embraced by undesired affections
of yellow-orange flame;
her visitor a hot-blooded drifter
who cares not for consent.

Octopus tentacles of grey smoke
do their Riverdance
through once-pine-scented air.
Nothing remains of the homestead.
Erect red planks now lie supine and black.

We say,
"We did not cause this"
as we flick our embers,
smoldering behind us.
And though we say, "We will survive,"

panicked feet beat a frenzied tempo,
clarions call for saviors on the hilltop.

Wake-up Call

Finches—or maybe warblers—
tweet their woodwind opus,

announce another morning's birth.
Newly-opened eyes repel optimism,

preferring to shrink from light,
but regalia of avian alerts

ignites flickering embers of optimism.
In this melodic moment I defy

the screeched pronouncements
of domineering corvids

who wish to drown in dissonance
my now embittered memories of sonic honey.

Post-Diluvian Love Poem

The hurried river,
mulligatawny-turbid,
slaps steep embankments,
beats impertinent walls,
gathers oak limbs as it moves.

See, through frosted glass,
this kaleidoscopic rain.
Chapped hands intertwined
We abandoned patron saints
for memory's keloid scars.

Now should be our time.
Did we not wait patiently?
But as the wind wails,
buffeting the tin roof's edge,
synchronous rhythms console.

Noctalgia

Lampposts and satellites
spill shiny dross into the black void,
jaundicing Heaven's infinite belly.

Photons, ruthlessly flexible,
bend to unmask verity,
but out of place, enveil it.

Oh, reckless skyglow, hide away.
The barn owl and petrel need no hindrance,
nor I who live to rest in bone-black shadow.

Neon and halogens enthrall
but cover up the skin of eventide,
indecent in their careless concealment.

Bring back the stars of yesteryear.
Excessive gleam has banished them from view.

Endurance

The lodgepole pines wear rings of black
and nothing up above.
Skeletal sylvan bones rattle,
offering token resistance
to hot-handed summer bluster.

Ferns and moss have reconvened.
Ephemerals and mallow sprout.
Below and beyond bark and phloem,
a rhizome revolution foments
under a nutritious ashen veil.

Thunderstroke disrupts the quiet greenwood.
Its newborn canopy shall fear no spark.

Fermata #4

Quicksand sucks our frenzied limbs,
yet we must lie still,
awaiting unknown saviors
in the heavy mire.

About the Author

Mukund Gnanadesikan is the author of the 2020 novel **Errors of Omission**, the 2023 poetry chapbook **Petit Morts: Meditations on Love and Death**, and the 2023 children's book **Clarence and Elroy**. His poetic influences include Langston Hughes, Rabindranath Tagore, Louise Glück, and Jericho Brown. When not writing, he practices medicine in California.